Dedicated to our daughters

...and to all kids in bilingual households learning to speak with Mommy, Papi, grandparents, abuelos, aunts and uncles, tíos y tías, cousins, primos, friends y amigos.

You are amazing!
¡Eres increíble!

Scan here for the read-along video.

Mommy says "family."

Papi dice "familia."

Mommy says "house."
Papi dice "casa."

 Mommy says "Good morning."

 Papi dice "Buenos días."

Mommy says "breakfast."
Papi dice "desayuno."

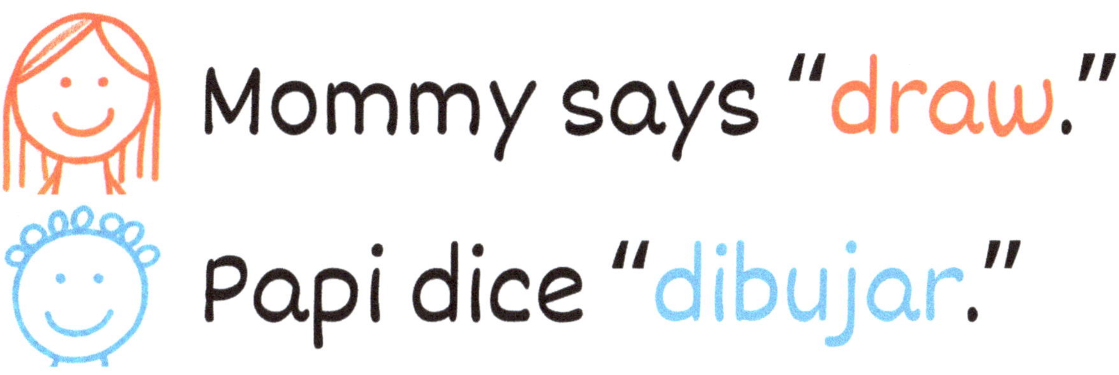

Mommy says "draw."
Papi dice "dibujar."

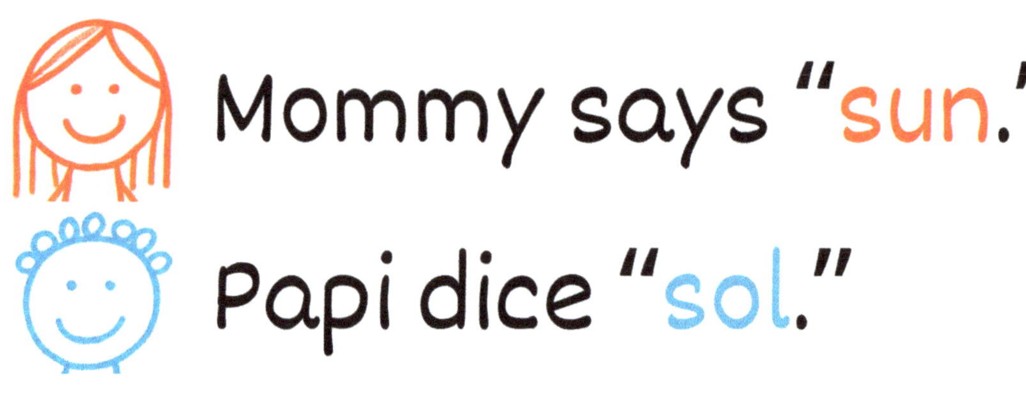

Mommy says "sun."
Papi dice "sol."

Mommy says "tree."

Papi dice "árbol."

Mommy says "flowers."
Papi dice "flores."

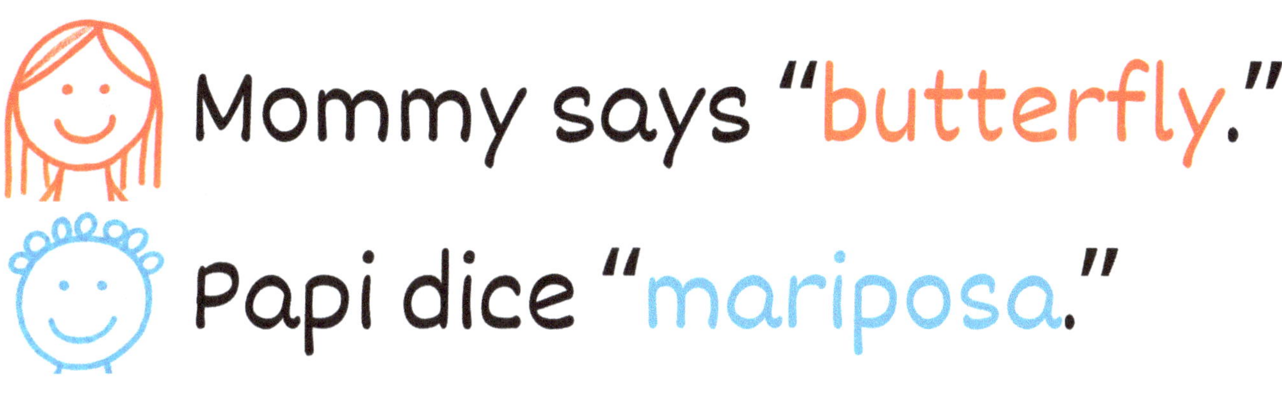

Mommy says "butterfly."
Papi dice "mariposa."

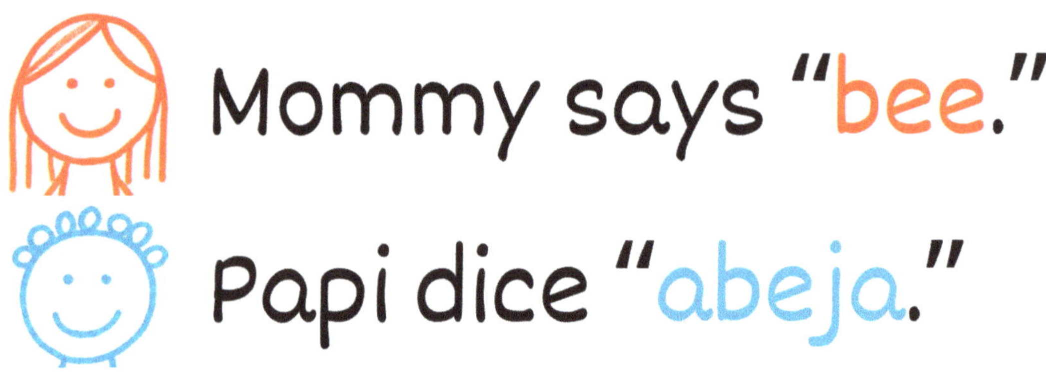

Mommy says "bee."

Papi dice "abeja."

Mommy says "bird."
Papi dice "pájaro."

Mommy says "airplane."

Papi dice "avión."

Mommy says "car."
Papi dice "carro."

 Mommy says "dog."

Papi dice "perro."

Mommy says "cat."

Papi dice "gato."

Mommy says "walk."
Papi dice "caminar."

Mommy says "park."

Papi dice "parque."

 Mommy says "play."

Papi dice "jugar."

 Mommy says "friends."

Papi dice "amigos."

 Mommy says "lunch."

 Papi dice "almuerzo."

Mommy says "music."

Papi dice "música."

 Mommy says "nap."

 Papi dice "siesta."

 Mommy says "dinner."

 Papi dice "cena."

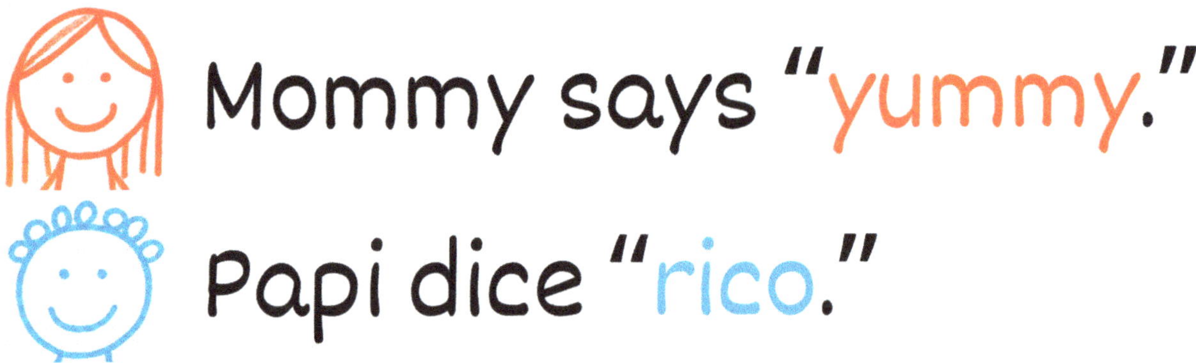

Mommy says "yummy."
Papi dice "rico."

Mommy says "moon."

Papi dice "luna."

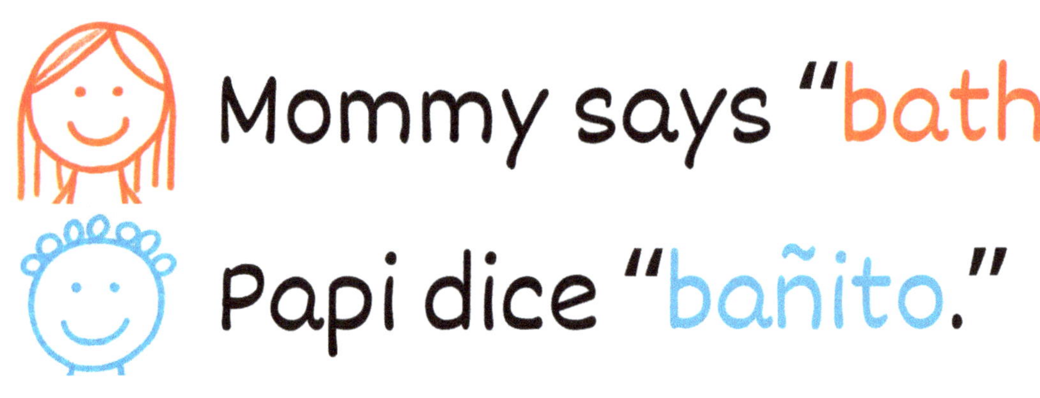

Mommy says "bath."

Papi dice "bañito."

Mommy says "book."
Papi dice "libro."

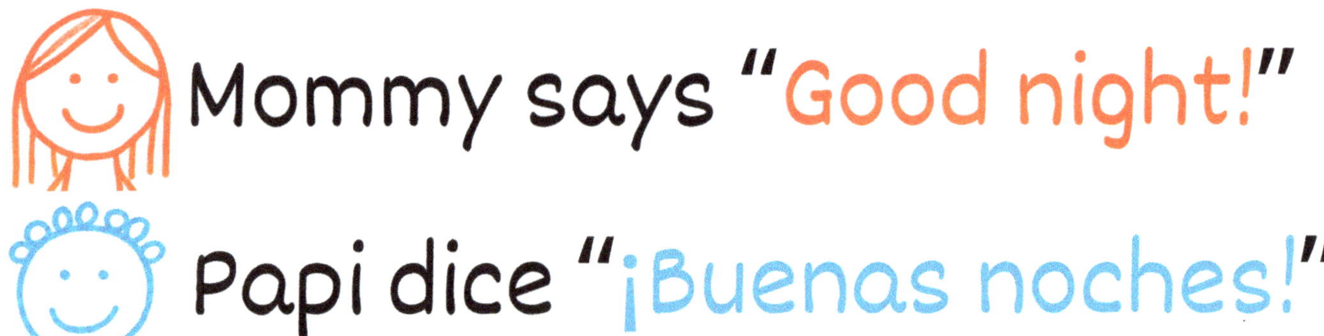

Mommy says "Good night!"

Papi dice "¡Buenas noches!"

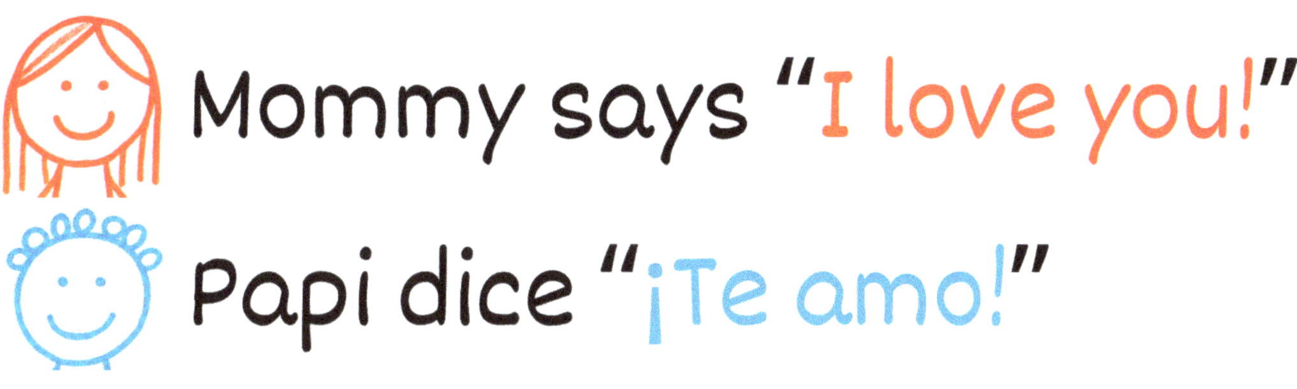

Mommy says "I love you!"
Papi dice "¡Te amo!"

ABOUT US

From Our Family to Yours 

We are Kallie and Joel, bilingual parents to two daughters who are learning both English and Spanish at home.

Kallie is a Spanish teacher with over 10 years of experience and the creator of Classes by Kallie, a line of digital resources, workbooks, and children's books that help teachers and parents teach Spanish at school or at home.

Joel is a native Spanish speaker and provides recordings for our resources to help students, parents, and children hear and practice pronunciation.

This book was inspired by a game we play with our oldest, quizzing her to see if she can identify whether words are in English or Spanish.

"Mommy says... ¿Qué dice Papi?" and "Papi dice... What does Mommy say?" are phrases we often use at home, and our daughter's face lights up when she remembers the word Mommy or Papi uses. Try it with your own words at home!

We hope this book brings a little extra joy to your storytime and helps spark a love of language learning. Be sure to visit our Amazon store for more books coming soon!

¡Disfruten y diviértense!
Kallie & Joel

TPT Store

Amazon Author Page

Mommy says... Papi dice...

www.ingramcontent.com/pod-product-compliance
Lightning Source LLC
Chambersburg PA
CBHW040220110726
48005CB00019B/3100